glug glug

glug glug

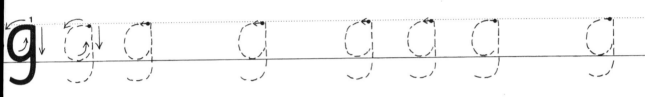

g g g g g g g g g

g g g g g g g g

g g g g g g g

Capital

plu___

___ift

fro___

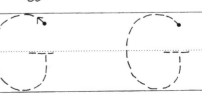

G G G G

3

By standing on the shelf,
Inky can reach the switch.
She can turn the light on
and off, *o, o, o, o, o, o.*

O o

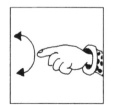

Action: Pretend to turn light switch on and off
and say *o, o, o, o.*

4

Write your name.

The sink is blocked.
When the water runs away it makes
a glugging, gurgling sound *g, g, g.*

Action: Spiral hand down, as if water going down the drain and say *g, g, g.*

2

on off on off

o

O

Capital

_ctopus

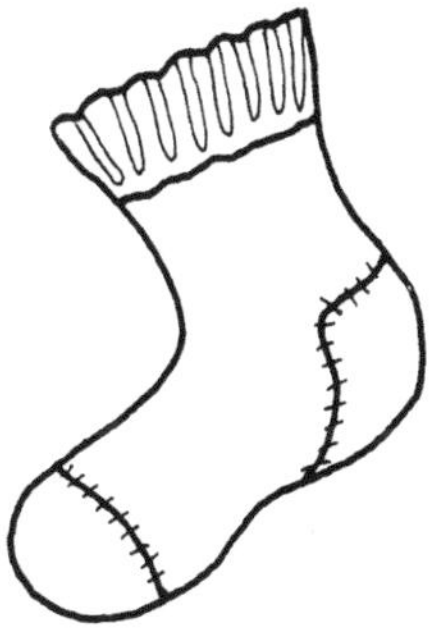

r_bin

s_ck

5

Bee has a new umbrella. She puts it up in the rain *u, u, u, up umbrella.*

U u

Action: Pretend to be putting up an umbrella and say *u, u, u, u.*

6

up umbrella

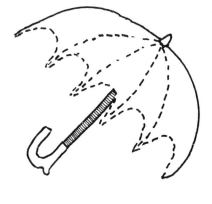

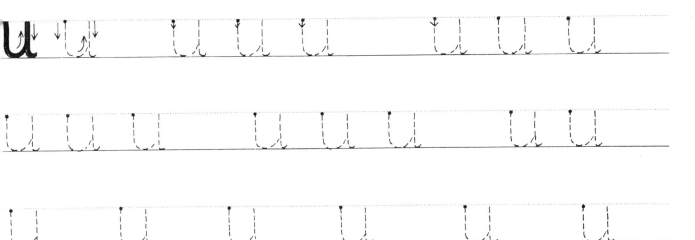

u

Capital

.__p

s__n

dr__m

7

L l

Snake is licking a lovely lemon lollipop *l, l, l.*

Action: Pretend to lick a lollipop and say *l, l, l, l.*

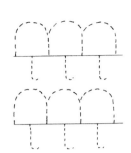

lick a lollipop

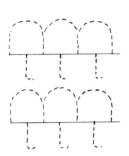

lick a lollipop

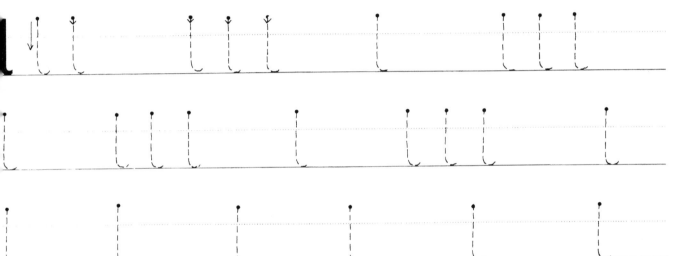

_emon

umbre__a

hi___

Capital

Ff

Snake thinks the inflatable fish is real and tries to catch it. His sharp teeth puncture it and it makes a *ffffff* sound as it goes flat.

Action: Let hands gently come together as if fish deflating and say *ffffff*.

flat fish

flat fish

f f f f f f f f f

f f f f f f f

f f f f f f

__lag

__rog

o____

F

Capital

Inky, Snake, and Bee are playing bat and ball in the park.

B b

Action: Pretend to hit a ball with a bat and say *b, b, b, b.*

bat and ball

bat and ball

b b b b b b b b

b b b b b b b b

b b b b b b

ra _ _ it

_ i _

cra _

Capital

B B B B B B

Some words are tricky and cannot be sounded out.

Here is a way of learning them.

Look	FOLD	**Cover**	FOLD	**Write, Check**	**Have another go**
Say the letters.		Try writing them.			

the | the | _____ | _____

are | are | _____ | _____

you | you | _____ | _____

Fill in the missing letters.

the   ar_   y_u

a_e   t_e   _re

yo_   th_   _ou

Match the small letters to the capitals.

Practice of the 'o' shape.
Put the patterns on the snakes.

Now check you know these sounds.
Write the letter. Draw a picture of something that begins with it.

a	h	l
t	r	u
s	c	k f
n	d	o
i	e	b
p	m	g

How quickly can you say them?

Fill in the missing sound.

b _ g

h _ n

b _ s

d _ g

c _ p

p _ g

w _ b

p _ n

s _ n

Read the words in the logs. Match each word to the picture in the frog that rhymes with it.

fun

red

mat

big

grab

log

When two letters making the same sound come next to each other you only say the sound once - r̤a̤b̤b̤i̤t̤.

Read each word and draw a picture of it.

rabbit

kitten

dress

hill

duck

parrot

Choose the word and write it underneath.

met mat man   log dig dog   cup cut cap

m a t

_ _ _   _ _ _

peg egg pig   net nut not   and ant act

_ _ _   _ _ _   _ _ _

hen hat pen   bin bus bug   sub sit sun

_ _ _   _ _ _   _ _ _

Write each word and read it. Then draw a picture of it.

hat	pen	ant
ink	man	cap
bed	dog	bus

Numbers need correct formation too.

Workbook 3 - Number 3)

1   2   3

Count the caterpillars.

3 3 3 3 3 3

Find the 3 caterpillars.

three three three

23

Activity

Flat fish race

Cut a fish shape from a piece of newspaper. Use another piece of paper folded into a fan to fan your fish along.

Mobile

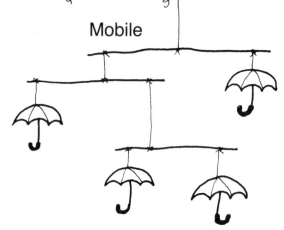

Cut some umbrella shapes from card. Draw them and hang them as a mobile.

Lemon ice cubes

Make some lemon ice cubes with a lemon drink put into an ice cube mould.

Read the story of the Three Billy Goats Gruff.